Mary Ellen Ciganovich is followed in our clinic with a history of epilepsy and multiple sclerosis. Ms. Ciganovich's positive outlook and wonderful spirit are a great inspiration. In addition, her knowledge and willingness to share has been of great help to me and I have been fortunate enough to pass on some of this information to other patients with these difficult diseases. I believe the book she has written, *Healing Words: Life Lessons to Inspire*, reflects the positive attitude which she has taken towards life's difficult challenges. It is a thoughtful and sensitive book that will touch many people.
—Jonathan Richman, M.D.

healing words
_____

Sincerely with Love,
Mary Ellen

healing words

LIFE LESSONS TO INSPIRE

Mary Ellen Ciganovich

TATE PUBLISHING & *Enterprises*

Healing Words
Copyright © 2010 by Mary Ellen Ciganovich. All rights reserved.

No part of this publication may be reproduced, stored in a retrieval system or transmitted in any way by any means, electronic, mechanical, photocopy, recording or otherwise without the prior permission of the author except as provided by USA copyright law.

The opinions expressed by the author are not necessarily those of Tate Publishing, LLC.

Published by Tate Publishing & Enterprises, LLC
127 E. Trade Center Terrace | Mustang, Oklahoma 73064 USA
1.888.361.9473 | www.tatepublishing.com

Tate Publishing is committed to excellence in the publishing industry. The company reflects the philosophy established by the founders, based on Psalm 68:11,
"The Lord gave the word and great was the company of those who published it."

Book design copyright © 2010 by Tate Publishing, LLC. All rights reserved.
Cover design by Rebekah Garibay
Interior design by Joey Garrett

Published in the United States of America

ISBN: 978-1-61739-151-4
Poetry / Inspirational & Religious
10.11.12

for my Father...

Acknowledgments

To all of the people who have supported me in my life and in the writing of this book—Thank You! I would like to give a special word of thanks to God, Jesus Christ, and all of his angels.

To My husband Peter, you encourage me to live the life I was meant to live, love unconditionally, and learn the lessons I need to learn. I love you and cherish every day that we have together!

My daughter, Stephanie, even though you are grown and on your own, you are always in my heart. I love you and I am very proud of you!

And to Baby Doll, my cat, for sitting patiently by my side!

Table of Contents

How This Book Can Help You	15
Awareness	18
Fear	19
God	20
Trust	21
Doing	22
Motives	23
Knowing	24
Meditate	25
Spirit	26
Getting	27
Society	28
Ego	29
Intimacy	30
Unconditional Love	31
Wholeness	32
The Journey	33

Expectations	34
Abundance	35
Thought	36
Becoming	37
Lack	38
Struggle	39
Truth	40
Friends	41
Rapture	42
Violence	43
Disease/Sickness	44
Past	45
Gratitude	46
Motives #2	47
Judgment	48
Wishing/Hoping	49
Worry	50
Stoppers	51
Knowings	52
Sin	53
Arguments	54
Resistance	55
Willingness	56

Death	57
Realness	58
Motivation	59
Prayer	60
Accidents	61
Soul	62
Detox	63
Choices	64
Differences/Expectations	65
Risk	66
Mirrors	67
Awareness #2	68
Upset	69
Gossip	70
Perfection	71
Things	72
Present Moment	73
Two Emotions	74
Beliefs	75
Of Like Minds	76
Listening	77
Visualize	78
Assumptions	79

Judgments	80
Good	81
Family	82
Truth #2	83
Perception	84
Real	85
God #2	86
Love	87
Joy	88
Frustration	89
Anger	90
Awakening	91
Letting Go	92
Faith	93
Miracles	94
Forgiveness	95
Bibliography	97
A Special Note of Thanks	101
About the Author	103

How This Book Can Help You

This book will support you in your journey toward finding the peace you are seeking. It is dedicated to all people who strive hard every day to learn God's lessons and purposes for their being on this plane of life. It will give you the insights you need to be able to see things differently. You will then be able to understand why you keep doing the same things over and over again. "Healing Words" will inspire you to look inside yourself, for that is where all of your answers reside.

Each page contains one of the "Life Lessons" that I have learned through many years of experiences, some of which were not pleasant. I thank *God* every day for allowing me to go through those hardships, because that is when I learned these truths that I can now pass on to you.

You should read the book through completely the first time. It is an easy book to read and was constructed this way on purpose so you will be able to digest the valuable material that will unfold throughout these pages.

Then put it down. Rest your mind and allow your soul to contemplate the words you have read.

In the morning, during your quiet time, pick the *Healing Words* text up and simply flip to any page. Read this life lesson one, two, or even three times. Meditate upon how this life lesson applies to you. As you go through your day, keep these words with you and learn the lesson you need to learn from your situations. In this way, you will not have to keep going through the same issues time after time after time.

There is nothing out there—either medically or psychologically—that you cannot heal yourself. You are in control and *you* are the one who can truly become a miracle worker when *you* choose to see things differently. Doctors and psychologists have their place in our society. These people can help you only to the extent that you *know* they can help you. *You* must pave the way for their success.

I have lived through many misperceptions in my life and have come through them healthy, whole, and happy because I choose to allow God to speak to me and I choose to listen!

I hope you will allow me to share with you these healing words and life lessons that have so changed my life for the better. I also hope you will incorporate the principles that work for you into your life and risk sharing with other people these healing words.

I sincerely hope you not only read these words but you listen to them through your heart. The messages are clear as I have translated them as I heard them. My wish is for you to hear these messages and continue on your journey to live through love, giving back to others what you have learned. For "As we give so shall we receive," and wouldn't the world be a much better place if everyone were at peace with themselves?

Sincerely with Love,
Mary Ellen Ciganovich

Awareness

Awakening to the
truth inside of
you is
awareness.
Becoming enlightened
to your own
errors is
awareness.
Walking through
your fears instead of
hiding from them is
awareness.
This becomes the first
and most important step
in your spiritual journey.

Amen.

Fear

Fear runs you.
You hide from your
fears and
you allow them to control you.
Fear is your answer
for everything that
you did not
accomplish in your life.
Ask yourself,
Why did I allow these
False
Expectations
Appearing
Real
to control me?
This is a wasted life.
Don't waste even one precious moment of life!

Amen.

God

God is
not only
out there!
This universal
power is inside of
you, and you, and you,
and every living thing
on this planet.
God made you
to live, learn, and love.
Your human thinking keeps
you from
living, learning, and loving.
Pity you don't live your life *now*
so you can learn your lessons
and love like you were meant
to love.

Amen.

Trust

Trust
that everything is
exactly as it
is supposed to be.
Trust
that something
good always
comes out of
every situation.
Trust
in life.
Trust
in love.
First you must
trust
yourself!

Amen.

Doing

Why aren't
you doing
what you love to do?
Fear?
Money?
Do what you love to do
and
the money will come!
Trust yourself!
Trust
the true spirit
inside yourself!
Do what you
love to do!
Be Happy!

Amen.

Motives

Look carefully
at your
motives.
You who do
good deeds
for others all the while
saying quietly to yourselves,
"If I do this for you,
then
what will you do for me?"
Truth comes from
the heart.
No motives.
Just goodness!
Just unconditional love!

Amen.

Knowing

You know
in your
soul
your truth.
You know
and
you don't
pay attention.
Listen to
your knowing.
Follow
your truth.
Be at peace.

Amen.

Meditate

Be quiet
and
meditate.
Release your past,
your troubles, your fears.
Relax,
and feel the pain of
it all being lifted from
your shoulders.
Reflect
on the lessons
you have learned
and listen as you meditate.
God speaks when
you do not!
Be quiet and listen to God!

Amen.

Spirit

Your spirit is
in truth
what you are.
Your loving,
kind,
generous spirit.
Stay out of
your humanness
and get into
your spirit.
Be what
you were meant
to be.
Get in touch with your heart,
your spirit, and
become awake!

Amen.

Getting

Interestingly enough
there
really is no
such word as "Get!"
Yet humans
use it or misuse it
all the time.
Stop the "getting"
and
begin giving to others.
In so doing,
you will be
giving
to yourself
and "getting"
eternal peace and happiness.

Amen.

Society

Society is a consciousness that
you as a group choose.
Come together and choose
love,
peace,
and happiness.
Your planet will then "out-picture" with
love,
peace,
and happiness.
The power you have within each of you is endless
and the power you have as a group consciousness is
indefinable!
Become one within yourselves and what you seek
as a societal group—your powers, your peace—
shall know no boundaries!

Amen.

Ego

Ego keeps you locked in
your house of unawareness.
You believe ego
protects you from feeling
the pain that comes
with truth.
Ego is *not* the protector from pain
but the root cause of
all human suffering!
Drop your egos, your false pretenses.
Come with love
—Unconditional Love—
and you will begin to
become aware
of the peace that
you hide inside yourself!

Amen

Intimacy

Intimacy is
what everyone says
they are searching for
in relationships.
Why do you hide your truths
from each other?
Allow your partner to see into you.
Let go and
in
to
me
see!
Then you will find true intimacy.
Then you will find a peaceful, loving,
relationship!

Amen.

Unconditional Love

Real love is
love without conditions,
or expectations,
or motives,
or reasons.
Real love is
unconditional.
It is like truth.
It just is.
No reasons.
No motives.
No conditions.
Just pure "Christ-like," God inspired
Love!

Amen.

Wholeness

You already
have everything
You will ever
need.
You already
know everything
you will ever need
to know.
You already are
the person you need
to become.
You just don't know it!
Wake up
to your
wholeness and
begin your life!

Amen.

The Journey

You are on your journey.
Will you learn
your lessons
this time?
Or
will you stay
in your ego state
and refuse?
Stubborn, controlling
human that you are.
If you make
that choice,
I guess you will just
have to come back and
begin the journey
again!

Amen.

Expectations

Get out of expectations.
Do things only out of love.
Why do anything expecting
to get a
"thank you" and
gratitude back?
Then don't do it in the first place!
Your expectations
get you into trouble.
Then you project these misperceptions
on the people around you. In reality
You are the one expecting them
to be a certain way.
Expect nothing—get everything!
Expect everything— get nothing!
That is the way of the universe;
that is God's way!

Amen.

Abundance

Everywhere on this planet
there is abundance.
Where you see lack; there is abundance.
The misperception is that
you are seeing incorrectly.
Have you truly
ever lacked for any "thing"?
No matter what you went through,
didn't you find every "thing" you
needed when you really needed it?
Maybe when you didn't have
some "thing" you actually didn't
want it or need it?
The abundance you seek
is inside you,
in your heart and
within your soul!

Amen.

Thought

Take no thought
for anything—for anyone.
Thinking
from the "ego state" brings trouble.
Thinking starts
Wars,
Murders,
Robberies,
Divorces!
Anything bad that you blameon anyone else, or God,
is not from anyone else, or God,
it is from your ownhuman thinking.
Stay *now*.
Stay happy.
Take *no* thought!

Amen.

Becoming

You have to
become
that which you seek.
You will find outside yourself
only the characteristics
that you possess
inside yourself.
If you want
respect
become respectful
to yourself,
to others,
to everyone you meet
and
what you become
you will finally find.

Amen.

Lack

Lack is nowhere.
Lack is
inside of you
when you fail to see clearly.
Stop projecting lack
onto those people
you supposedly
love so dearly.
That is not
love.
That is projecting
disgusting thoughts
from your human mind.
Lack is not loving.
Therefore, lack is not real!
Lack is man-made.

Amen.

Struggle

The struggle
is not
required.
Humans try
to make life
hard
when it is
so easy,
so simple.
You must
let life
be
easy,
as it was
meant to
be.

Amen.

Truth

Truth is always
sour
in the mouth
and sweet
in the belly.
Lies are always
sweet
in the mouth
and sour
in the belly.
This is why it is
painful and hard
to look at the truth
about yourself and it is
always so easy to see the
truth about others!

Amen.

Friends

You think your friends teach you
lessons, and they do.
However your "enemies" teach you
the lessons that are hardest for you
to swallow.
So you dismiss them and don't
want them in your life, thinking
that you can run away or
hide from learning your
hard lessons.
When has anyone been able to run
away or hide from God?
God will find you and send someone
new to teach you the same lesson.
God has to because
God wants you to be happy—Really happy!
Learn your lessons. Choose happiness!

Amen.

Rapture

The heavens shall open
and the rapture
shall begin.
If you have
learned your lessons
and lived wisely
you will be ready.
If you haven't
then you are continually
being given chances
to choose again.
Choose wisely
and learn.
Be ready for the rapture!

Amen.

Violence

Violence is
a fearful
act.
Violence is
not
loving.
Therefore violence
is
not a reality
of God.
Man
chooses
to make it real!

Amen.

Disease/Sickness

Disease is an illusion
of the mind.
When you are not
"at ease" with your life,
then a disease will appear
to assist you in learning all
of the lessons you need to
Learn while on
this plane of life.
Learn that you are as healthy
as you want to be.
You are in control! Stop giving away
Your power to others!
You are your physician!
"Heal thyself" and
"To thine own self be true."

Amen.

Past

The past
does not exist.
It is gone.
Why are you
stuck in a time
caught up
in memories
of pain that
never was or will be?
The past
and the
future
are simply
your perceptions of what you
think.
"Take no thought!"

Amen.

Gratitude

Take nothing
for
granted!
Become grateful.
Generate
an "attitude of gratitude"
for life,
for love
for yourself.
Then you may
"live life to the fullest."
Smile
and
become grateful!

Amen.

Motives #2

You must deny
your motives.
Stop the lies. Stop the pretense.
Come from love.
No expectations and no motives.
Even when you think
your actions are
coming from
good intentions or motives,
think again!
Is ANY motive a good motive?
Or
is it just your human attempt
to justify
an untruth?
Think about it!

Amen.

Judgment

When you place
blame on others
you are judging
them.
When you see
someone else as not
up to your standards,
you are judging them.
In truth you are the one
who is not up to
standard.
Who are you to judge
or be judged?
The peace in you
knows no judgments.
Have peace!

Amen.

Wishing/Hoping

All you need already exists.
Your wishes have
already been granted.
Your dreams have
already been accomplished.
The true misperception
lies in the simple fact
that you "think" there is
something you need to wish for!
There is no wish
you can wish,
no hope
you can hope,
no dream you can dream
that is not already a reality!

Amen.

Worry

No amount of worry
about any situation
ever changed the
outcome of that situation.
Worry only
creates stress, tension,
headaches,
and other disorders.
Why do you insist on
worrying when you
know in truth
that "worry" does no
good at all?
Worry is a "no" thing.
Stop creating that
which doesn't exist!

Amen.

Stoppers

Humans use many stoppers.
Words such as
"I think…"
"I guess…"
"If only…"
"But…"
"What if…"
Drop these words
and say the sentence again.
Now your true meaning
will be clear
and you will
have said exactly
what you meant to say
in the first place.

Amen.

Knowings

You worry about
Things…
Places…
People…
Events…
that you don't know will
ever affect you! Your human mind
attempts to figure everything
out and put it in a nice, neat,
wrapped-up box, when you don't know the box
even exists!
Know that nothing exists
that you don't want to exist!
Know your "knowings."
Always stay with your "knowings."
Stay with "*all*"!

Amen.

Sin

Have you ever
missed your
mark?
Then you have
sinned.
Learn from it
go
forward
and
hit the bull's eye!

Amen.

Arguments

Arguments get you
nowhere, especially
since you are
not really arguing
with anyone
other than yourself!
Look into the mirror.
Argue at yourself.
Because it is not
"what goes into your mouth
that defiles you" rather
"what comes out of your mouth
that defiles you."
To an extent you
cannot ever recover.
Be careful!

Amen.

Resistance

Resistance will gain you nothing!
You assume by hiding
your fears, they
will go away or disappear.
Your fears will come
around again
in some other form of disguise.
It will be an attempt
by the universe/God
to get you to learn!
When you walk through your
fears and learn from your fears
they will disappear!
What you resist will persist
until you let go and learn!

Amen.

Willingness

Become willing
to see things
differently.
Become willing
to be open
and
learn from life.
Become willing
to make
different choices.
Become willing
to see your path
toward the light.
God will be with you
now and always.

Amen.

Death

In truth
there is no death.
Your energy will
simply
change form.
Your human form
will be gone
and your true essence,
your soul,
your spirit,
will know—as it has always
known—
the peace
that you have strived
to reach while
on this earthly plane.

Amen.

Realness

Get real!
Feel your feelings.
They will
lead you toward
your truth. Become
Really
Enthusiastic
About
Life
And know your truth.
The only one who can truly take
care of you is
you!
Stop looking for someone
else to do the things
that only you can do!

Amen.

Motivation

Motivate yourself!
Stop giving yourself
reasons
for getting zero
results.
Don't depend on
others
for what
you can already do!
You know
you can do it all
yourself.
Motivation,
the driver is *you!*

Amen.

Prayer

Some of you don't ever
have time for God. And
God
always has time for you.
Some of you have
specified times for
Prayer,
like morning and night.
You should pray
constantly, consistently.
You should pray without
ceasing for prayer is how
you talk to God.
With your prayers shall come
your peace.
Become peaceful. Pray!

Amen.

Accidents

No accidents exist
in this world.
Accidents are simply
God's universal wake-up
calls for you to look inside
yourself and learn. Every incident,
every place,
every person
has a purpose—
all good,
all loving,
all real.
Learn the lessons you refuse
to learn and accidents will
cease to surround you.
Achieve your purpose! Do it *now*!

Amen.

Soul

We are all one
spirit
of
unified
life.
We are all of one
spirit.
We are all of one
soul.
To be prejudiced against one
means to be prejudiced
against all,
even yourself.
Become one with each other,
one loving true
spirit, one soul.

Amen.

Detox

Mentally, you must
detox.
Mentally, you
must cleanse yourself
of all that society
has attempted to
teach you.
It will be awkward.
It will be difficult.
It will
become
the most worthwhile
experience
of your life!

Amen.

Choices

Your life is a reflection
of the choices
you have made
up to that moment.
You have been blessed
with the ability
to choose.
If you don't like your life,
stop making the same choices
over … and over … and over
again
expecting different results.
A red stove will always
be hot when you touch it!
Choose differently! Choose wisely!
Choose again!

Amen.

Differences/Expectations

Why do I
expect you
to be different
when you can't?
You probably don't
even know how.
And
maybe, just maybe,
I really don't want you to be!
Only I can change,
in order for my
"Perceptions"
to change.
I must be
different—
not you!

Amen.

Risk

Reach inside yourself
and risk!
It is through
risking all
that you lose
nothing
and gain everything.
If you risk nothing
then you shall lose
everything
and gain nothing.
It is in risking that you
grow, learn, and become closer
to the peace you seek.
Reach inside yourself
and *risk!*

Amen.

Mirrors

Friends,
family,
bosses,
co-workers,
your entire world
is a mirror
of you!
If you
don't like
something that
you see
in the mirror,
change yourself!

Amen.

Awareness #2

Becoming aware
is painful
and is the first step
you must take
to become
who you really are.
It's like living in
a darkened room and
seeing the light
for the first time.
Your eyes hurt.
That is awareness.
It hurts.
Feel the pain.
Feel the fear.
Walk through it
and go forward.

Amen.

Upset

You are never
upset for the
reason
you think.
Whatever you think
you are upset
with
is simply your
"Ego" protecting its
precious self from
a truth that is so
painful for you to bear.
Ask yourself," What am
I afraid of?"
Then the "truth "
for your upset
will become clear.

Amen.

Gossip

Your humanness talks of what others have done.
"Can you believe it?
"I would never!"
"Did you hear?"
In doing this, you are only demeaning yourself.
Gossip does not build you up,
it tears you down.
It is one of the root misperceptions in life.
Why do you defile yourself while
you also defile others?
Gossip is far away from
Love.
Gossip is so far away from
God.
Why do you go so far away from God
when you want to be so close?
Interesting?

Amen.

Perfection

You are perfect
just the way you are.
There is nothing to fix.
There is nothing to complete.
You are not your
job,
body,
clothes,
car
or anything else that your
"humanness" and society makes important.
If you were,
then when those
things aren't,
where are you?
Think about it!

Amen.

Things

Place importance not
on things.
For no "thing" is as
important as
your true loving goodness
toward your fellow
human
or
your loving attitude
toward
yourself.
Things are "nothings!"
You
are
Very
Special!

Amen.

Present Moment

Become aware
of
the present moment.
In truth
that is all you have.
Enjoy it!
Love it!
Learn to live "now" and "here"
or you will live being
"nowhere."

Amen.

Two Emotions

Only two emotions exist:
Fear or Love.
Your choice.
You can stay victims
of all your little fears
or you can face them
with a loving attitude
and change.
Choose wisely!

Amen.

Beliefs

What you believe is
not necessarily true
and what is true should
not always be believed.
Look inside yourself.
Get in touch with what
you know
not
what you believe.
A belief always
includes
at least one doubt
and
a knowing
is
a
truth!

Amen.

Of Like Minds

We are all
of like minds
when we become aware
of the truth in life.
Wake up!
Become aware
of the light
inside you
and
you will begin to see
the light inside others!
We are all one
body, soul, and
spirit.
We are all
of like minds!

Amen.

Listening

Everybody thinks
they are
listening to each other.
Actually,
you are just
trying to figure out
what you will say next
in order to prove
your point!
Listen
from your heart.
Listen!
All of the answers
will be provided.
God speaks when you don't!

Amen.

Visualize

See what you want to be.
People not sighted
see the truth
quicker, clearer
only because their egos
and their thinking selves
stay out of the way.
Close your eyes and
visualize your path
exactly
as you want it to be.
It will become
just the way you see it.
You truly will *see* it
only
when you believe it to be
your truth.

Amen.

Assumptions

Ninety-nine percent of all assumptions
are false!
You assume one thing
when
really another is true.
Then you say to each other
"Well, I thought…"
or
"I just knew you would…"
Speak clearly
and listen
to
yourself.
Assume nothing!

Amen.

Judgments

Be careful
how you judge others.
In truth
you are
only judging yourself.
Who are you to
condemn and criticize?
"Judge not least ye be judged."

Amen.

Good

The good that you see in others
is the good
that is inside of you!
The things about others
that irritate you
are God's way
—the universe's way—
of
showing you
what you need
to work on in yourself!
This can be the best
gift God can give us.
It is all in the way "*you*"
perceive it!

Amen.

Family

My family is non-supportive.
I keep trying to
make a family
where there is none.
Why do I expect things
to change?
Why do I expect them
to be different?
Expectations lead to fears and
fears lead to negative self-talk.
I am in control
and
I choose
to have no expectations
of this non-family.
Therefore, being let down
is not a possibility!

Amen.

Truth #2

Truth is.
That is simple enough.
When I stay in the
"*now*"
and feel my feelings
working only on
myself,
blaming you for nothing,
projecting nothing at
you,
then I am here
and
there is truth.

Amen.

Perception

Your world is
as you perceive it to be.
If you perceive a hurtful, angry
world
Then you must be a hurtful, angry
person.
If you want to change your
world,
you must first
change yourself.
Feel the anger. Feel the hurt.
Feel the fear. Walk through it.
Begin
to perceive the world
you are in
as a loving, peaceful place!

Amen.

Real

Only love is real.
Nothing unreal exists.
Herein lies the peace of God.
Herein lies the peace of
all mankind.
Peace be with you.
Now and always,
Go with God.

Amen.

God #2

God is in me.
God is in you.
God is the loving force that
is felt around the world.
You must call upon the power of God
within you
to guide you through your
feelings and fears.
You must walk through your pain,
in order to get
to the other side.
You will get there!
Actually, in truth,
you already are there—
now!

Amen.

Love

I love you.
How can I, when I find it
so hard to love myself?
I want so much for you
to care about me
and make me special.
First I must feel special about myself!
This is very hard work!
Nothing worthwhile is ever easy and
you are very worthwhile
to me.
Now I must become worthwhile
to myself!
Then true love
Unconditional love
will be shared between us.

Amen.

Joy

I feel joy when I do what I
love to do.
I think I feel joy when you pay
attention to me
and we talk.
Possibly, that is the "false joy"
of the "ego."
Am I looking at you to fix me,
to make me complete?
There is nothing to fix.
I am already
complete!

Amen.

Frustration

There is nothing to be
frustrated with
that I don't project into
my own little world.
These things are as I see them
not as they really are.
Aah—
That *is* the frustration!

Amen.

Anger

I am angry
with you.
No, with myself.
I am projecting it at you
to save myself.
In doing that,
I lose myself.
So I must face the anger,
and feel the pain.
I will walk through my fears
to become
a more peaceful and more loving
human being.

Amen.

Awakening

Awaken
to the
present moment.
Awaken
to your
true spiritual self.
Awaken
to the
"real world"
of love.
Awaken!
Arise and see,
truly see,
your glowing light
of love!

Amen.

Letting Go

Let go
of your fears.
You hear the phrase,
"let go and let God."
The phrase should say,
"letting go is letting God"
take control of
the life
God
has created for you
to enjoy.
Give up your human
"ego" control
and
Allow God to work through you.
Let go of the past. Let go of
your misperceptions about life!

Amen.

Faith

Faith is your foundation.
Faith is your freedom.
Have faith and free your fears.
Faith is...
something you just do,
something you just accept.
It is a result of finding
within yourself a part
of God's loving consciousness, which
surrounds all of us.
You will find faith
in your goodness,
in your heart of hearts,
in your knowings,
and in your soul.
You cannot see faith and without it
you will be forever blind.

Amen.

Miracles

Miracles are natural occurrences
that happen every day.
A miracle happens
every time you
change your perceptions
and
begin to see things
differently!
Miracles come from
having faith.
Miracles come from
our one loving true God
and
miracles come from
within you!
Change your perceptions.
Create a miracle!

Amen.

Forgiveness

Forgiveness
is the key to becoming
R.E.A.L.
(Really Enthusiastic About Life)
Forgive
your past,
your present,
yourself,
and go forward
into the light.
Bringing love,
peace,
and harmony
to the world.
Better hurry—
it's almost
too late!

Amen.

Bibliography

God, His Son Jesus Christ, and the Holy Spirit

The Holy Bible: All Versions

The Course of Miracles

All spirituality teachers who have touched my life.

Thank you and Amen.

Mary Ellen

A Special Note of Thanks

As I struggled to find just the right title for this book, God led me to speak to a group of people at the Hara Foundation in Southern Pines, North Carolina. Tom Thompson, the leader of the foundation, called this group Healing Words. It was an excellent group of people who were all on their own spiritual journeys.

Upon completion of this book, I thought that I might take it to the Healing Words group to see what their opinion was of the completed text. It was at that moment that I realized the book should be titled "Healing Words." It was clear to me that God's very purpose for me to speak to that group was not for them; it was for me; as God always gives back to you what you give to God.

I want to thank Tom Thompson of the Hara Foundation in Southern Pines, North Carolina, and the Healing Words group for supporting me on my own spiritual journey.

Sincerely with love,
Mary Ellen

About the Author

Mary Ellen was born in Batavia, New York, and moved to Atlanta, Georgia, when she was four years old. She attended Tucker High School and graduated Magna Cum Laude in Education from the University of Georgia. After graduating, she went on to teach middle school for over thirteen years in four different states.

Mary Ellen has one daughter, Stephanie, a graduate of Georgia State University in Atlanta and Midwestern University in Arizona. Stephanie is practicing emergency medicine as a Physician's Assistant in the Phoenix area.

As a child, Mary Ellen's family life was very dysfunctional, as there were many fights between her parents. She turned to God, his angels, and prayer to support her through these difficult times.

While in the first grade, Mary Ellen was diagnosed with epilepsy. She struggled with this throughout her childhood. During her early twenties, she began to study spirituality and holistic healing. Although always a student of the Bible, Mary Ellen now added "The Course in Miracles" to her studies. As she studied, she began to apply what she learned toward healing her own seizure disorder. Mary Ellen went on to become a speaker for the National Epilepsy Foundation.

Then in 1987, while living as a single mom in the Atlanta area, Mary Ellen was diagnosed with multiple sclerosis. Instead of falling victim to this diagnosis, she decided to learn once more how to fight this disorder through the use of spiritual and meditative techniques, herbs, vitamins, and exercise. This was over twenty-two years ago and today Mary Ellen is very healthy!

She lives with her husband, Peter, in Chattanooga, Tennessee. Mary Ellen conducts seminars called "Live, Love, and Learn," where she teaches people how to look truthfully at their own lives, take charge, and control their health through the use of doctors in combination with alternative medicine.

Visit her Web site:
www.askmaryellen.com or
e-mail her at askmaryellen@aol.com or write to:
Mary Ellen Ciganovich
PMB 573
Ooltewah, Tennessee 37363

Amen.